FRIENDS
OF ACF

D0098177

3 1833 02842 5

j811
Dickinson, Emily,
Poems for youth

ALLEN COUNTY PUBLIC LIBRARY
FORT WAYNE, INDIANA 46802

You may return this book to any location of
the Allen County Public Library.

DEMCO

4/96

Poems for Youth

EMILY DICKINSON

Poems for Youth

Illustrations by **Thomas B. Allen**

Edited by
Alfred Leete Hampson

Foreword by
May Lamberton Becker

Little, Brown and Company
Boston   New York   Toronto   London

Allen County Public Library
900 Webster Street
PO Box 2270
Fort Wayne, IN 46801-2270

Text copyright 1918, 1919, 1924, 1929, 1932, 1934
by Martha Dickinson Bianchi
Illustrations copyright © 1996 by Thomas B. Allen

All rights reserved. No part of this book may be reproduced in any form or by
any electronic or mechanical means, including information storage and
retrieval systems, without permission in writing from the publisher, except
by a reviewer who may quote brief passages in a review.

Second Edition

With two exceptions, all of the poems in this book appear in the Centenary
Edition of *The Poems of Emily Dickinson*, edited by Martha Dickinson Bianchi
and Alfred Leete Hampson and published by Little, Brown and Company. The
poem beginning "The Wind did not come from the orchard to-day" is from
Emily Dickinson Face to Face, by Martha Dickinson Bianchi, and the poem "Is
it true, dear Sue?" is from *The Life and Letters of Emily Dickinson*, by Madame
Bianchi, both reprinted by permission and special arrangement with Houghton
Mifflin Company, the authorized publishers.

Front cover signature: Courtesy of the Todd-Bingham Picture Collection, Yale
University Library.

Library of Congress Cataloging-in-Publication Data
Dickinson, Emily, 1830–1886.
  Poems for youth / Emily Dickinson ; edited by Alfred Leete Hampson ;
  foreword by May Lamberton Becker ; illustrations by Thomas B. Allen.
    p. cm.
  Summary: A collection of seventy-eight poems that highlight the seasons,
the passage of time, and reflect on life, written by one of America's foremost
poets.
  ISBN 0-316-18435-7
  1. Children's poetry, American. [1. American poetry.]
I. Hampson, Alfred Leete. II. Allen, Thomas B., ill. III. Title.
PS1541.A6 1996a
811'.4—dc20   95-33497

10 9 8 7 6 5 4 3 2 1
MV - NY
Published simultaneously in Canada
by Little, Brown & Company (Canada) Limited

Printed in the United States of America

Editor's Note

Three generations of Dickinsons lived together at Amherst in the two houses behind the high evergreen hedge— "The Mansion" and "The Other House," which still stand on the main street of the little college town.

And still the "little path just wide enough for two who love" runs across the green lawns from one door to another—past a garden of hollyhocks and roses in summer and a background of tall pines "upon a marge of snow" in winter.

The Mansion was the home of Emily Dickinson; and "a hedge away" at The Other House lived her only brother, Austin, and his wife, whom Emily Dickinson from girlhood had called her "Sister Sue," and their three children, Emily Dickinson's only niece and two nephews. It is in their home, now known as The Evergreens, that all her personal belongings are preserved.

To these three children she was not merely an aunt, but an enchanting playfellow, a confederate, an understanding friend—as long as she lived sending across the lawn to their mother and to them countless little notes and poems, from which those given here have been chiefly chosen.

Grateful recognition is due the many teachers and friends of young people who have urged such a collection, and especial thanks to Marion Dodd and Bertha Mahony Miller.

A. L. H.

FOREWORD

When I was younger than I am now, I spent my summers in northern New England, where there are pine forests. No one felled trees in the wood I knew best, but there were little clearings where long ago trees had fallen and been cleared away—sunlit circles hidden in the green. One day, parting the undergrowth in the direction of the light, I found myself on the rim of one of these little lost clearings, and there, all alone by itself, I saw my first scarlet lily. It stood straight as a flame, burning toward the sky.

I shall not forget the surprise it gave me. You would have looked for such a flower in the tropics, but here it was among the northern pines. You might have expected it in a greenhouse, or in some walled garden visited by hummingbirds, but here it was blazing only for the hermit thrush and sheltered only by the forest ring, all by itself, glad of itself, rising from brown mold and gray rock straight toward the sun.

Coming upon the poems of Emily Dickinson was like coming upon that scarlet flower. For I soon found that the red wood lily of New England belongs there just as much as the pines. Like them, it strikes root firmly into the soil, stands the strain of hard weather, and reaches up to the sky that belongs to everybody. So the strange blazing verse of Emily Dickinson is rooted in New England character and its bright color rises from our brown earth. Delicate as these verses are, they are robust and rich with life. That is why I am glad that a selection of them is now offered directly to young people, in whom life is rich and strong and robust.

You have no doubt heard that only a very few of her poems appeared in print in her lifetime, and then by no wish of hers. After her death—as you will learn from Madame Bianchi's *Life and Letters of Emily Dickinson*—these poems were dramatically discovered, and one slender volume of them appeared. Others followed at intervals; but it was forty years before her fame, smoldering all that time, burst into a worldwide blaze. You may wonder, as you discover these poems for yourself, why it took so long. That is partly because many of those who read them at first thought they broke the rules and forms of poetry. We care less for those forms and rules now. We have come to apply Emily Dickinson's own test:

If I read a book and it makes my whole body so cold no fire can ever warm me, I know it is poetry. If I feel physically as if the top of my head were taken off, I know this is poetry.

Poems that meet this test make forms and rules of their own. Hers did, in time. They were far ahead of their time. The one thing about Emily Dickinson that seems impossible is the fact that she was born more than a hundred years ago. For as you grow up, and as the generation after you grows up, Emily Dickinson will be waiting for you, and for them, ready to slip into your life these messages of hers, as she used to slip into the hand of her "Sister Sue" the bits of paper with some of these verses on them — silently, sure that the one who gets them will understand.

For these are messages. They go straight from her life into yours, direct as telegrams. That is one reason why they are so short. She wrote, not for fame or for money, but because she had something to say that must be said, and she knew that nothing like that is really said at all until it is said in poetry. After that, no one can say it again in a different way; he can only quote the poem.

Let me repeat something I have said elsewhere: "Poetry is the most direct way of saying anything. It deals with the very nature of things and goes straight to it. We are not used to such dizzying directness: We make great argument, about it and about — and while we are arguing through pages of prose, a poem has given us the essence of the idea in two perfect lines." Emily Dickinson has given us more lines like that than any other poet of our time. Reading them is like letting the genie out of the bottle: The meaning fills the whole sky.

If all this makes you want to know more about the circumstances of her life, Madame Bianchi's books will fascinate you. And Emily's own poems will give you what mattered most in life to her — and through that, perhaps a key to the house of life itself.

May Lamberton Becker
New York City
September 17, 1934

Poems for Youth

THERE is no frigate like a book
  To take us lands away,
Nor any coursers like a page
  Of prancing poetry.

This traverse may the poorest take
  Without oppress of toll;
How frugal is the chariot
  That bears a human soul!

I'M nobody! Who are you?
Are you nobody, too?
Then there's a pair of us — don't tell!
They'd banish us, you know.

How dreary to be somebody!
How public, like a frog
To tell your name the livelong day
To an admiring bog!

⊰ 3 ⊱

SOME keep the Sabbath going to church;
I keep it staying at home,
With a bobolink for a chorister,
And an orchard for a dome.

Some keep the Sabbath in surplice;
I just wear my wings,
And instead of tolling the bell for church,
Our little sexton sings.

God preaches, — a noted clergyman, —
And the sermon is never long;
So instead of getting to heaven at last,
I'm going all along!

(Sent to her little niece, who was left in her care on Sunday mornings before she was old enough to go to church.)

THE Sea said "Come" to the Brook,
The Brook said "Let me grow!"
The Sea said "Then you will be a Sea—
I want a brook, Come now!"

I like to see it lap the miles,
And lick the valleys up,
And stop to feed itself at tanks;
And then, prodigious, step

Around a pile of mountains,
And, supercilious, peer
In shanties by the sides of roads;
And then a quarry pare

To fit its sides, and crawl between,
Complaining all the while
In horrid, hooting stanza;
Then chase itself down hill

And neigh like Boanerges;
Then, punctual as a star,
Stop—docile and omnipotent—
At its own stable door.

(The Train)

Hope is the thing with feathers
That perches in the soul,
And sings the tune without the words,
And never stops at all,

And sweetest in the gale is heard;
And sore must be the storm
That could abash the little bird
That kept so many warm.

I've heard it in the chillest land,
And on the strangest sea;
Yet, never, in extremity,
It asked a crumb of me.

THE Heart is the capital of the Mind,
The Mind is a single State;
The Heart and the Mind together make
A single continent.

One—is the population—
Numerous enough;
This ecstatic nation
Seek—it is Yourself.

Nature is what we see,
The Hill, the Afternoon—
Squirrel, Eclipse, the Bumble-bee,
Nay—Nature is Heaven.

Nature is what we hear,
The Bobolink, the Sea—
Thunder, the Cricket—
Nay,—Nature is Harmony.

Nature is what we know
But have no art to say,
So impotent our wisdom is
To Her simplicity.

Not knowing when the dawn will come
  I open every door;
Or has it feathers like a bird,
  Or billows like a shore?

I'LL tell you how the sun rose,—
A ribbon at a time.
The steeples swam in amethyst,
The news like squirrels ran.

The hills untied their bonnets,
The bobolinks begun.
Then I said softly to myself,
"That must have been the sun!"

. . . .

But how he set, I know not.
There seemed a purple stile
Which little yellow boys and girls
Were climbing all the while,

Till when they reached the other side,
A dominie in gray
Put gently up the evening bars,
And led the flock away.

A MURMUR in the trees to note,
    Not loud enough for wind;
A star not far enough to seek,
    Nor near enough to find;

A long, long yellow on the lawn,
    A hubbub as of feet;
Not audible, as ours to us,
    But dapperer, more sweet;

A hurrying home of little men
    To houses unperceived,—
All this, and more, if I should tell,
    Would never be believed.

Of robins in the trundle bed
    How many I espy
Whose nightgowns could not hide the wings,
    Although I heard them try!

But then I promised ne'er to tell;
    How could I break my word?
So go your way and I'll go mine,—
    No fear you'll miss the road.

THE Duties of the Wind are few—
To cast the Ships at sea,
Establish March,
The Floods escort,
And usher Liberty.

DEAR March, come in!
How glad I am!
I looked for you before.
Put down your hat—
You must have walked—
How out of breath you are!
Dear March, how are you?
And the rest?
Did you leave Nature well?
Oh, March, come right upstairs with me,
I have so much to tell!

I got your letter, and the bird's;
The maples never knew
That you were coming,—I declare,
How red their faces grew!
But, March, forgive me—
And all those hills
You left for me to hue;
There was no purple suitable,
You took it all with you.

Who knocks? That April!
Lock the door!
I will not be pursued!
He stayed away a year, to call
When I am occupied.
But trifles look so trivial
As soon as you have come,
That blame is just as dear as praise
And praise as mere as blame.

Pink, small, and punctual,
Aromatic, low,
Covert in April,
Candid in May,

Dear to the moss,
Known by the knoll,
Next to the robin
In every human soul.

Bold little beauty,
Bedecked with thee,
Nature forswears
Antiquity.

(With the first arbutus)

❧ 15 ❧

So bashful when I spied her,
So pretty, so ashamed!
So hidden in her leaflets,
Lest anybody find;

So breathless till I passed her,
So helpless when I turned
And bore her, struggling, blushing,
Her simple haunts beyond!

For whom I robbed the dingle,
For whom betrayed the dell,
Many will doubtless ask me,
But I shall never tell!

PERHAPS you'd like to buy a flower?
But I could never sell.
If you would like to borrow
Until the daffodil

Unties her yellow bonnet
Beneath the village door,
Until the bees, from clover rows
Their hock and sherry draw,

Why, I will lend until just then,
But not an hour more!

THE robin is the one
That interrupts the morn
With hurricd, few, express reports
When March is scarcely on.

The robin is the one
That overflows the noon
With her cherubic quantity,
An April but begun.

The robin is the one
That speechless from her nest
Submits that home and certainty
And sanctity are best.

A DROP fell on the apple tree,
Another on the roof;
A half a dozen kissed the eaves,
And made the gables laugh.

A few went out to help the brook,
That went to help the sea.
Myself conjectured, Were they pearls,
What necklaces could be!

The dust replaced in hoisted roads,
The birds jocoser sung;
The sunshine threw his hat away,
The orchards spangles hung.

The breezes brought dejected lutes,
And bathed them in the glee;
The East put out a single flag,
And signed the fête away.

IT will be Summer eventually—
Ladies with parasols,
Sauntering gentlemen with canes,
And little girls with dolls

Will tint the pallid landscape
As 'twere a bright bouquet,
Though drifted deep in Parian
The village lies to-day.

The lilacs, bending many a year,
Will sway with purple load;
The bees will not despise the tune
Their forefathers have hummed;

The wild rose redden in the bog,
The aster on the hill
Her everlasting fashion set,
And covenant gentians frill,

Till summer folds her miracle
As women do their gown,
Or priests adjust the symbols
When sacrament is done.

THE bee is not afraid of me,
I know the butterfly;
The pretty people in the woods
Receive me cordially.

The brooks laugh louder when I come,
The breezes madder play.
Wherefore, mine eyes, thy silver mists?
Wherefore, O summer's day?

THE wind tapped like a tired man,
And like a host, "Come in,"
I boldly answered; entered then
My residence within

A rapid, footless guest,
To offer whom a chair
Were as impossible as hand
A sofa to the air.

No bone had he to bind him,
His speech was like the push
Of numerous humming-birds at once
From a superior bush.

His countenance a billow,
His fingers, if he pass,
Let go a music, as of tunes
Blown tremulous in glass.

He visited, still flitting;
Then, like a timid man,
Again he tapped—'twas flurriedly—
And I became alone.

A SEPAL, petal, and a thorn
Upon a common summer's morn,
A flash of dew, a bee or two,
A breeze
A caper in the trees, —
    And I'm a rose!

Two butterflies went out at noon
And waltzed above a stream,
Then stepped straight through the firmament
And rested on a beam;

And then together bore away
Upon a shining sea, —
Though never yet, in any port
Their coming mentioned be.

If spoken by the distant bird,
If met in ether sea
By frigate or by merchantman
Report was not to me.

THE grass so little has to do,—
A sphere of simple green,
With only butterflies to brood,
And bees to entertain,

And stir all day to pretty tunes
The breezes fetch along,
And hold the sunshine in its lap
And bow to everything;

And thread the dews all night, like pearls,
And make itself so fine,—
A duchess were too common
For such a noticing.

And even when it dies, to pass
In odors so divine,
As lowly spices gone to sleep,
Or amulets of pine.

And then to dwell in sovereign barns,
And dream the days away,—
The grass so little has to do,
I wish I were a hay!

THE Wind did not come from the orchard today,
Further than that,—
Nor stop to play with the hay,
Nor threaten a hat.
He's a transitive fellow, very—
Rely on that.

If he leave a burr at the door,
We know he has climbed a fir,—
But the fir is where? Declare—
Were you ever there?
If he brings odours of clovers,
And that is his business not ours,
He has been with the mowers,
Whetting away the hours
To sweet pauses of hay—his way
Of a June day.

If he fling sand and pebble,
Little boys' hats and stubble,
With an occasional steeple,
And a hoarse "Get out of the way, I say!"
Who'd be the fool to stay? Would you?
Say, would you be the fool to stay?

A NARROW fellow in the grass
Occasionally rides;
You may have met him,—did you not?
His notice sudden is.

The grass divides as with a comb,
A spotted shaft is seen;
And then it closes at your feet
And opens further on.

He likes a boggy acre,
A floor too cool for corn.
Yet when a child, and barefoot,
I more than once, at morn,

Have passed, I thought, a whip-lash
Unbraiding in the sun,—
When, stooping to secure it,
It wrinkled, and was gone.

Several of nature's people
I know, and they know me;
I feel for them a transport
Of cordiality;

But never met this fellow,
Attended or alone,
Without a tighter breathing,
And zero at the bone.

(The Snake)

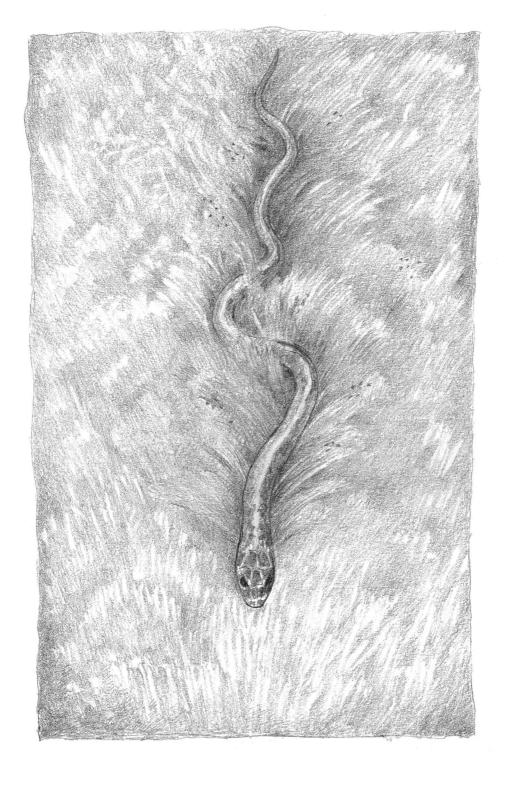

Could I but ride indefinite,
　　As doth the meadow-bee,
And visit only where I liked,
　　And no man visit me,

And flirt all day with buttercups,
　　And marry whom I may,
And dwell a little everywhere,
　　Or better, run away

With no police to follow,
　　Or chase me if I do,
Till I should jump peninsulas
　　To get away from you,—

I said, but just to be a bee
　　Upon a raft of air,
And row in nowhere all day long,
　　And anchor off the bar,—
What liberty! So captives deem
　　Who tight in dungeons are.

A FUZZY fellow without feet
Yet doth exceeding run!
Of velvet is his countenance
And his complexion dun.

Sometimes he dwelleth in the grass,
Sometimes upon a bough
From which he doth descend in plush
Upon a passer-by.

All this in summer—
But when winds alarm the forest folk,
He taketh damask residence
And struts in sewing silk.

Then, finer than a lady,
Emerges in the spring,
A feather on each shoulder—
You'd scarce accredit him.

By men yclept a caterpillar—
By me—but who am I
To tell the pretty secret
Of the Butterfly!

LIKE trains of cars on tracks of plush
I hear the level bee:
A jar across the flower goes,
Their velvet masonry

Withstands until the sweet assault
Their chivalry consumes,
While he, victorious, tilts away
To vanquish other blooms.

His feet are shod with gauze,
His helmet is of gold;
His breast, a single onyx
With chrysoprase, inlaid.

His labor is a chant,
His idleness a tune;
Oh, for a bee's experience
Of clovers and of noon!

THE pedigree of honey
Does not concern the bee;
A clover, any time, to him
Is aristocracy.

≪ 31 ≫

The spider as an artist
   Has never been employed,
Though his surpassing merit
   Is freely certified

By every broom and Bridget
   Throughout a Christian land
Neglected son of genius,
   I take thee by the hand

WITHIN my garden rides a bird
Upon a single wheel,
Whose spokes a dizzy music make
As 'twere a traveling mill.

He never stops, but slackens
Above the ripest rose,
Partakes without alighting,
And praises as he goes;

Till every spice is tasted,
And then his fairy gig
Reels in remoter atmospheres,
And I rejoin my dog.

And he and I perplex us
If positive 'twere we —
Or bore the garden in the brain
This curiosity?

But he, the best logician,
Refers my duller eye
To just vibrating blossoms
An exquisite reply!

(This poem is about the hummingbirds in her garden.)   43

The wind begun to rock the grass
With threatening tunes and low, —
He flung a menace at the earth,
A menace at the sky.

The leaves unhooked themselves from trees
And started all abroad;
The dust did scoop itself like hands
And throw away the road.

The wagons quickened on the streets,
The thunder hurried slow;
The lightning showed a yellow beak,
And then a livid claw.

The birds put up the bars to nests,
The cattle fled to barns;
There came one drop of giant rain,
And then, as if the hands

That held the dams had parted hold,
The waters wrecked the sky,
But overlooked my father's house,
Just quartering a tree.

S WEET is the swamp with its secrets,
    Until we meet a snake;
'Tis then we sigh for houses,
    And our departure take
At that enthralling gallop
    That only childhood knows.
A snake is summer's treason,
    And guile is where it goes.

I KNOW some lonely houses off the road
A robber'd like the look of,—
Wooden barred,
And windows hanging low,
Inviting to
A portico,

Where two could creep:
One hand the tools,
The other peep
To make sure all's asleep.
Old-fashioned eyes,
Not easy to surprise!

How orderly the kitchen'd look by night,
With just a clock,—
But they could gag the tick,
And mice won't bark;
And so the walls don't tell,
None will.

A pair of spectacles ajar just stir—
An almanac's aware.
Was it the mat winked,
Or a nervous star?
The moon slides down the stair
To see who's there.

There's plunder,—where?
Tankard, or spoon,
Earring, or stone,
A watch, some ancient brooch
To match the grandmamma,
Staid sleeping there.

Day rattles, too,
Stealth's slow;
The sun has got as far
As the third sycamore.
Screams chanticleer,
"Who's there?"

And echoes, trains away,
Sneer—"Where?"
While the old couple, just astir,
Think that the sunrise left the door ajar!

I STARTED early, took my dog,
And visited the sea;
The mermaids in the basement
Came out to look at me,

And frigates in the upper floor
Extended hempen hands,
Presuming me to be a mouse
Aground, upon the sands.

But no man moved me till the tide
Went past my simple shoe,
And past my apron and my belt,
And past my bodice too,

And made as he would eat me up
As wholly as a dew
Upon a dandelion's sleeve —
And then I started too.

And he — he followed close behind:
I felt his silver heel
Upon my ankle, — then my shoes
Would overflow with pearl.

Until we met the solid town,
No man he seemed to know;
And bowing with a mighty look
At me, the sea withdrew.

'TWAS such a little, little boat
That toddled down the bay!
'Twas such a gallant, gallant sea
That beckoned it away!

'Twas such a greedy, greedy wave
That licked it from the coast;
Nor ever guessed the stately sails
My little craft was lost!

WHETHER my bark went down at sea,
Whether she met with gales,
Whether to isles enchanted
She bent her docile sails;

By what mystic mooring
She is held to-day,—
This is the errand of the eye
Out upon the bay.

I T tossed and tossed,—
A little brig I knew,—
O'ertook by blast,
It spun and spun,
And groped delirious, for morn.

It slipped and slipped,
As one that drunken stepped:
Its white foot tripped,
Then dropped from sight.

Ah, brig, good-night
To crew and you;
The ocean's heart too smooth, too blue,
To break for you.

AN everywhere of silver,
With ropes of sand
To keep it from effacing
The track called land.

A BIRD came down the walk:
He did not know I saw;
He bit an angle-worm in halves
And ate the fellow, raw.

And then he drank a dew
From a convenient grass,
And then hopped sidewise to the wall
To let a beetle pass.

He glanced with rapid eyes
That hurried all abroad,—
They looked like frightened beads, I thought
He stirred his velvet head

Like one in danger; cautious,
I offered him a crumb,
And he unrolled his feathers
And rowed him softer home

Than oars divide the ocean,
Too silver for a seam,
Or butterflies, off banks of noon,
Leap, plashless, as they swim.

To make a prairie it takes a clover and one bee,—
And revery.
The revery alone will do
If bees are few.

HIGH from the earth I heard a bird;
　He trod upon the trees
As he esteemed them trifles,
　And then he spied a breeze,
And situated softly
　Upon a pile of wind
Which in a perturbation
　Nature had left behind.
A joyous-going fellow
　I gathered from his talk,
Which both of benediction
　And badinage partook,
Without apparent burden,
　I learned, in leafy wood
He was the faithful father
　Of a dependent brood;
And this untoward transport
　His remedy for care,—
A contrast to our respites.
　How different we are!

THE Robin's my criterion of tune
Because I grow where robins do—
But were I Cuckoo born
I'd swear by him,
The ode familiar rules the morn.
The Buttercup's my whim for bloom
Because we're orchard-sprung—
But were I Britain-born
I'd daisies spurn—
None but the Nut October fits,
Because through dropping it
The seasons flit, I'm taught.
Without the snow's tableau
Winter were lie to me—
Because I see New Englandly.
The Queen discerns like me—
Provincially.

GOD made a little gentian;
It tried to be a rose
And failed, and all the summer laughed.
But just before the snows
There came a purple creature
That ravished all the hill;
And summer hid her forehead,
And mockery was still.
The frosts were her condition;
The Tyrian would not come
Until the North evoked it.
"Creator! shall I bloom?"

(The Blue Gentian, the last flower of the year)

As children bid the guest good-night,
And then reluctant turn,
My flowers raise their pretty lips,
Then put their nightgowns on.

As children caper when they wake,
Merry that it is morn,
My flowers from a hundred cribs
Will peep, and prance again.

Whose are the little beds," I asked,
"Which in the valleys lie?"
Some shook their heads, and others smiled,
And no one made reply.

"Perhaps they did not hear," I said;
"I will inquire again.
Whose are the beds, the tiny beds
So thick upon the plain?"

" 'Tis daisy in the shortest;
A little farther on,
Nearest the door to wake the first,
Little leontodon.

" 'Tis iris, sir, and aster,
Anemone and bell,
Batschia in the blanket red,
And chubby daffodil."

Meanwhile at many cradles
Her busy foot she plied,
Humming the quaintest lullaby
That ever rocked a child.

"Hush! Epigea wakens!
The crocus stirs her lids,
Rhodora's cheek is crimson, —
She's dreaming of the woods."

Then, turning from them, reverent,
"Their bed-time 'tis," she said;
"The bumble-bees will waken them
When April woods are red."

(The Bed-time of the Flowers)

W<small>HEN</small> they come back,
If blossoms do—
I always feel a doubt
If blossoms can be born again
When once the art is out.

When they begin,
If Robins may—
I always had a fear
I did not tell, it was their last
Experiment last year.

When it is May,
If May return—
Had nobody a pang
Lest on a face so beautiful
He might not look again?

If I am there—
One does not know
What party one may be
Tomorrow,—but if I *am* there
I take back all I say!

THE morns are meeker than they were,
The nuts are getting brown;
The berry's cheek is plumper,
The rose is out of town.

The maple wears a gayer scarf,
The field a scarlet gown.
Lest I should be old-fashioned,
I'll put a trinket on.

Blazing in gold and quenching in purple,
Leaping like leopards to the sky,
Then at the feet of the old horizon
Laying her spotted face, to die;

Stooping as low as the kitchen window,
Touching the roof and tinting the barn,
Kissing her bonnet to the meadow,—
And the juggler of day is gone!

(*Sunset*)

THE mountains grow unnoticed,
Their purple figures rise
Without attempt, exhaustion,
Assistance or applause.

In their eternal faces
The sun with broad delight
Looks long—and last—and golden,
For fellowship at night.

SHE sweeps with many-colored brooms,
And leaves the shreds behind;
Oh, housewife in the evening west,
Come back, and dust the pond!

You dropped a purple ravelling in,
You dropped an amber thread;
And now you've littered all the East
With duds of emerald!

And still she plies her spotted brooms,
And still the aprons fly,
Till brooms fade softly into stars—
And then I come away.

(Autumn Sunset)

How the old mountains drip with sunset,
 And the brake of dun!
How the hemlocks are tipped in tinsel
 By the wizard sun!

How the old steeples hand the scarlet,
 Till the ball is full,—
Have I the lip of the flamingo
 That I dare to tell?

Then, how the fire ebbs like billows,
 Touching all the grass
With a departing, sapphire feature,
 As if a duchess pass!

How a small dusk crawls on the village
 Till the houses blot;
And the odd flambeaux no men carry
 Glimmer on the spot!

Now it is night in nest and kennel,
 And where was the wood,
Just a dome of abyss is nodding
 Into solitude!—

These are the visions baffled Guido;
 Titian never told;
Domenichino dropped the pencil,
 Powerless to unfold.

❧ 54 ❧

THE Ones that disappeared are back,
The Phoebe and the Crow,
Precisely as in March is heard
The curtness of the Jay—
Be this an Autumn or a Spring?
My wisdom loses way,
One side of me the nuts are ripe—
The other side is May.

❧ 55 ❧

WHO robbed the woods,
The trusting woods?
The unsuspecting trees
Brought out their burrs and mosses
His fantasy to please.
He scanned their trinkets, curious,
He grasped, he bore away.
What will the solemn hemlock,
What will the fir-tree say?

(The Wind in Autumn)

I reckon, when I count at all,
First Poets—then the Sun—
Then Summer—then the Heaven of God—
And then the list is done.
But looking back—the first so seems
To comprehend the whole—
The others look a needless show,
So I write Poets—All.
This summer lasts a solid year,
They can afford a sun
The East would deem extravagant,
And if the final Heaven
Be beautiful as they disclose
To those who trust in them,
It is too difficult a grace
To justify the dream.

THE sky is low, the clouds are mean,
A travelling flake of snow
Across a barn or through a rut
Debates if it will go.

A narrow wind complains all day
How some one treated him;
Nature, like us, is sometimes caught
Without her diadem.

It sifts from leaden sieves,
It powders all the wood,
It fills with alabaster wool
The wrinkles of the road.

It makes an even face
Of mountain and of plain,—
Unbroken forehead from the east
Unto the east again.

It reaches to the fence,
It wraps it, rail by rail,
Till it is lost in fleeces;
It flings a crystal veil

On stump and stack and stem,—
The summer's empty room,
Acres of seams where harvests were,
Recordless, but for them.

It ruffles wrists of posts,
As ankles of a queen,—
Then stills its artisans like ghosts,
Denying they have been.

THESE are the days that Reindeer love
And pranks the Northern star,
This is the Sun's objective
And Finland of the year.

FOLLOW wise Orion
Till you lose your eye,
Dazzlingly decamping
He is just as high.

ARCTURUS is his other name,—
I'd rather call him star!
It's so unkind of science
To go and interfere!

I pull a flower from the woods,—
A monster with a glass
Computes the stamens in a breath,
And has her in a class.

Whereas I took the butterfly
Aforetime in my hat,
He sits erect in cabinets,
The clover-bells forgot.

What once was heaven, is zenith now.
Where I proposed to go
When time's brief masquerade was done,
Is mapped, and charted too!

What if the poles should frisk about
And stand upon their heads!
I hope I'm ready for the worst,
Whatever prank betides!

Perhaps the kingdom of Heaven's changed!
I hope the children there
Won't be new-fashioned when I come,
And laugh at me, and stare!

I hope the Father in the skies
Will lift his little girl,—
Old-fashioned, naughty, everything,—
Over the stile of pearl!

◆§ 62 §◆

GOD permits industrious angels
Afternoons to play.
I met one,—forgot my school-mates,
All, for him, straightway.

God calls home the angels promptly
At the setting sun;
I missed mine. How dreary marbles,
After playing Crown!

◆§ 63 §◆

LIGHTLY stepped a yellow star
To its lofty place,
Loosed the Moon her silver hat
From her lustral face.
All of evening softly lit
As an astral hall—
"Father," I observed to Heaven,
"You are punctual."

THE moon was but a chin of gold
    A night or two ago,
And now she turns her perfect face
    Upon the world below.

Her forehead is of amplest blond;
    Her cheek like beryl stone;
Her eye unto the summer dew
    The likest I have known.

Her lips of amber never part;
    But what must be the smile
Upon her friend she could bestow
    Were such her silver will!

And what a privilege to be
    But the remotest star!
For certainly her way might pass
    Beside your twinkling door.

Her bonnet is the firmament,
    The universe her shoe,
The stars the trinkets at her belt,
    Her dimities of blue.

How still the bells in steeples stand,
　　Till, swollen with the sky,
They leap upon their silver feet
　　In frantic melody!

ONE Sister have I in our house,
And one a hedge away,
There's only one recorded
But both belong to me.

One came the way that I came
And wore my last year's gown,
The other as a bird her nest,
Builded our hearts among.

She did not sing as we did,
It was a different tune,
Herself to her a music
As Bumble-bee of June.

To-day is far from childhood,
But up and down the hills
I held her hand the tighter,
Which shortened all the miles.

And still her hum the years among
Deceives the Butterfly,
Still in her eye the Violets lie
Mouldered this many May.

I spilt the dew but took the morn,
I chose this single star
From out the wide night's numbers,
Sue—forevermore!

(Sent to her brother Austin's wife)

Is it true, dear Sue?
Are there Two?
    I shouldn't like to come
For fear of joggling Him!
If you could shut Him up
    In a coffee cup,
Or tie Him to a pin
Till I got in,
Or make Him fast
To Pussy's fist,
Hist! Whist!
    I'd come!

The Face we choose to miss,
Be it but for a day—
As absent as a hundred years
When it has rode away.

ALTER? When the hills do.
Falter? When the sun
Question if his glory
Be the perfect one.

Surfeit? When the daffodil
Doth of the dew:
Even as herself, O friend!
I will of you!

HE ate and drank the precious words,
His spirit grew robust;
He knew no more that he was poor,
Nor that his frame was dust.
He danced along the dingy days,
And this bequest of wings
Was but a book. What liberty
A loosened spirit brings!

HAVE you got a brook in your little heart,
Where bashful flowers blow,
And blushing birds go down to drink,
And shadows tremble so?

And nobody knows, so still it flows,
That any brook is there;
And yet your little draught of life
Is daily drunken there.

Then look out for the little brook in March,
When the rivers overflow,
And the snows come hurrying from the hills,
And the bridges often go.

And later, in August it may be,
When the meadows parching lie,
Beware, lest this little brook of life
Some burning noon go dry!

To fight aloud is very brave
But gallanter, I know,
Who charge within the bosom,
The cavalry of woe.

Who win, and nations do not see,
Who fail, and none observe,
Whose dying eyes no country
Regards with patriot love.

We trust, in plumed procession,
For such the angels go,
Rank after rank, with even feet
And uniforms of snow.

My soul accused me
And I quailed
As tongues of diamond
Had reviled.

All else accused me
And I smiled,
My soul that morning
Was my friend.

Her favor is the best disdain
Toward artifice of Time or men,
But her disdain — 'twere cooler bear
A finger of enameled fire!

❧ 74 ❧

I TOOK my power in my hand
And went against the world;
'Twas not so much as David had,
But I was twice as bold.

I aimed my pebble, but myself
Was all the one that fell.
Was it Goliath was too large,
Or only I too small?

❧ 75 ❧

A FACE devoid of love or grace,
A hateful, hard, successful face,
    A face with which a stone
Would feel as thoroughly at ease
As were they old acquaintances, —
    First time together thrown.

❧ 76 ❧

WHO has not found the heaven below
    Will fail of it above.
God's residence is next to mine,
    His furniture is love.

IF I can stop one heart from breaking,
I shall not live in vain;
If I can ease one life the aching,
Or cool one pain,
Or help one fainting robin
Unto his nest again,
I shall not live in vain.

I NEVER saw a moor,
I never saw the sea;
Yet know I how the heather looks,
And what a wave must be.

I never spoke with God,
Nor visited in heaven;
Yet certain am I of the spot
As if the chart were given.

INDEX